The author first took up writing when she was twelve and wrote this book when she was just sixteen years old. It is the first in a series of books that she hopes to publish in the future. She hopes that anyone who reads this book thoroughly enjoys it.

I want to dedicate this book to my mum and dad, for their inspiration and consistent help and support.

Fiona Estelle Clarke

CHASING RAINBOWS

AUSTIN MACAULEY PUBLISHERS™

LONDON · CAMBRIDGE · NEW YORK · SHARJAH

A CIP catalogue record for this title is available from the British Library.

ISBN 9781398433274 (Paperback)
ISBN 9781398433281 (ePub e-book)

www.austinmacauley.com

First Published 2022
Austin Macauley Publishers Ltd®
1 Canada Square
Canary Wharf
London
E14 5AA

I would like to thank my dad for helping me pick the title for my book, and my mum for all the inspiration she has given me.

Jobs

Sometimes when I go to the job Centre,
I am 17 or 18 and it is one to remember.

There is a sense of anticipation in the air,
Work starting, here and there.

Positive attitudes we have to be there at 8 or 9 o clock,
Right the way round, a twelve hour shift, tick toc.

Walking home or riding my bike, with a loaf of bread on the handlebars,
Watching out for buses, trucks and cars.

An old dirt track and in the bleak mid-winter atmosphere with my long honey blonde hair down to my waist,

A memory of when I was a young girl to cut and paste.
Instances that have happened throughout your time in this world,
Achievements that have been fulfilled.

Food

It's jumbled up inside us with other things, From spaghetti, to hoops and rings.

Food is many different types and sorts,
Some people have had given to them, some they have bought.

If you have food that is good for you, it may just be a dream,
You may not need wrinkle or little moisturizing cream.

You know that fruit and veg is good for you, It will make you big and strong, it will renew.

If you love this type of food that is all that you will need,
It is fine for the whole world to feed.

A Day to Remember

Maybe when you are grown up, perhaps have a husband or wife,
You look over your shoulder through the days of your life.

Little things come back to you, to your mind,
Poems, stories and it is a beautiful time that you will find.

It could be a special day like the start or finishing of your teens,
Something funny like when you fell over and tipped the beans.

Something flawless like putting shake and vac down or vacuuming up,
Having a drink, dinner, tea or sup.

Young Youth

Sometimes when I watch a children's adventure story like see
how they run or Mildred Hubble,
About the girl who is never out of trouble.

Listening to the teachers conversations and sticking up for the
pupils rights,
Breaking the school rules as she snoops around the sights.

Saving the day and finding out the truth,
It makes me wonder about young youth.

What it is like to have fun without getting caught,
Whether you're at home, school or where you are taught.

Led into mischief by her curiosity,
Like a spring that feeds her generosity.

So naturally pretty, humble and sweet,
Running through the woods with the grass swaying under her
feet.

Lighting up the countryside with her smile,
Knowing she will be at her grans in a little while.

Young youth, a time of mystery between childhood and
romance,
When everyone is given at least one chance.

A time of innocence when with purity she flows,
Like the summertime fruits or enchanted garden that grows.

Red lipped and fair skinned,
As fresh as the air of scented wind.

Running along to Sunday school and then back home,
Jumping into a bath of strawberries and foam.
Young youth a time when you are starting to notice changes
as you are getting washed and dressed,
A bit of hair and an uneven breast.

When you have stopped playing with your toys,
Started getting interested in boys.

Sneaking out to meet them and experiencing your first kiss,
There is nothing this girl won't miss.

Like a long lost dream as you see them running down passed
the garden and over by the pond,
With each other they are already getting fond.

Young youth, a time of enjoyment that could last forever,
till the next summer blows over,
Something you will remember when the meadow blossoms
and you smell the yellow clover.

When you see young boys and girls playing in the sun,
You will know it is their turn to have fun.

Harvest Time

Harvest time is like the sun rising over a ripe field,
When the corn is ready it will be picked and pealed.

When the time is right people will gather together all the grain,
What they have worked hard for all year till it comes round again.

Strawberries, grapes and baskets of bread,
As they listen in church for the sermon to be read.

Food will be given and songs will be sung,
Like hosanna and morning has broken.

About what it was really like on that very first day,
The wondrous awe that makes children want to play.

Plentiful in its richness, majestic in its beauty,
Harvest time always comes round bright and fruity.

It is the goodness you reap from what you have sown,
 The company you keep and the food you have grown.

It Is You, That Is Who

It is you, that is who that can wear all light colours and get a good job,
It is you, that is who that can eat healthy food and put it on the hob.

It is you, that is who that can send your children to college or university and give them the best start in life,
It is you, that is who that can guide them to being someone's husband or wife.

It is you, that is who that can have a record number of children and grandchildren if you start young and carry on,
It is you, that is who that can play your favorite music in the living years and sweet song.

It is you, that is who that can let your hair down and be a really happy person and live life to the full,
It is you, that is who that can go on to blossom and flourish and be as gentle as wool.

It is you, that is who that can make the most of being yourself whether you are a young girl, boy, woman or man,
It is you, that is who that can say the big yes and giant size I can.

Little Boy

There was a little boy who lived in this house,
He was quiet and tender as a mouse.

He was a cute, cuddly boy underneath, always casual smart,
Not too perfect, out with the cart.

He was a gentle, loving boy,
Always playing with his favorite toy.

He would play all day with a toy car,
His parents would not let him go far.

He was nearly a teenager and was always roller skating at random,
When he grew up, he was handsome.

Little Girl

There was a little girl who lived in this house, so pretty was
this one,
She glowed like the sun.

She had lovely long, thick hair of red,
A little brown bear that she called Ted.

A bit small for her age,
She had skin so tender and white as a schoolbook page.

She had hair down to her knees,
So it blew with the breeze.

She looked special and pure,
Growing fast, one day mature.

Courage

Proper yellow hearted courage, that's what it is,
Teenagers having boyfriends, it's the biz.

Skateboarding and out on their bikes, Buying paper,
cardboard and yikes.

Courage is like the sun rising in the morning on a field,
With the grass of green and the corn that will yield.

Fresh, ripe corn and shredded wheat and rice,
It is good for your heart and always tastes nice.

Courage with long blonde hair down to your waist,
New shoes and socks that are well laced.

Love Like Yours

Love like yours whispers around every rose that blooms,
It's the bases for life that makes up our fathers rooms.

When the day is still, people walk by and no one seems to care,
Love like yours sprays a heavenly sent through the air.

Love like yours comes from a heart that is pure,
Forever perfect it holds the key to mature.

Love like yours flows from Jesus into the world,
Helping every mind come to peace, every heart build.

If I had the choice of the world I would not have picked another,
Love like yours makes me proud to call you my mother.

Children of The Meadow

Children of the meadow, playing amongst the flowers that smell so sweet,
Children of the meadow, running through the grass with the sun glistening under their feet.

As it lights up their faces and shines through their hair,
You realize that they are not ordinary children, they are rosy and fair.

They are always happy because they are always nice to each other and make each other smile,
The purity that runs through them is cleaner than the Nile.

People have painted pictures of their happy times,
Poems, stories and nursery rhymes.

About their adventures in the place where they live,
With such a lot of beauty and so much to give.

Where the happy sent of summer wonder fills the air,
A place of mystery for adults and children alike to share.

A place where the sun never sets and you can play all day,
Surrounded with the peace of the meadow in a childlike way.

Where the grass is so green and the flowers are so yellow,
A light and peaceful place for everyone to mellow.

A child's dream of having gold at the end of a rainbow,
That nothing can ever spoil or stain bow.

Where the wondrous beauty and excitement will never end
and till the setting of the sun,
Where there is always time to be happy and have fun.

Birthdays

Sometimes when I think of birthdays it reminds me of pastel coloures, of different coloured cards and presents,
A birthday is for enjoying yourself, around every and all crescents.

Birthdays are a milestone in one more step along the world I go and moving on with God in your secular life,
Birthdays are a stage closer to going to heaven for all normal people, every body's husband and wife.

Birthdays are a from the old and to the new over many seconds, days and years,
Birthdays are for your nice niece and for a range of boyfriends and sirs.

Birthdays are a special time for 18 year old's and lots of young people, many nobles who are coming of age,
Birthdays are a time when you should celebrate, sing and appreciate your salary or wage.

Birthdays are a time when you are maybe starting a new college course or business,
Birthdays are a time to plan out your life, the rest of your days, ready to impress.

The Fairy Dust of Being a Child

Sometimes when its Christmas or I watch a good film like home alone or peter pan,

That brings out the child in you like only they can,
About the boy who never becomes a man.

I remember the fairy dust of being a child,
What it is like to jump around wild.

A film that jogs your imagination when you think you cannot remember,
It was not that long ago, just a few years last December.

When you could build tree houses in the garden and play games in the woods,
The merry men of Leicester and Robin Hoods.

When you could have little adventures of your own before going back to school the next day,
No one would know why you were so happy no way.

Singing to the sound of I have seen the golden sunshine and morning has broken,
With the fresh sent of summer were you awoken.

When you could look through your window on Easter or Christmas eve,
The wonder would come to life the more you believe.

The more you believe the more real it would seem,

Awaken from your sleep this is no dream.

A Place

There is a place as I look up in college, passed the bookshelf
to the window,
Where everything is sunny and life dwells between heaven
and earth limbo.

Time stands still in the peaceful oasis,
Surrounded by the cool air tied with white laces.

There is a place far away,
Where the doves swoop to enjoy the freshness of a new day.

Where the clouds float through the sky like peace's of ice
cream or cotton wool,
Pure tranquility in heaven so full.

Happy emotions that you would not find anywhere else in the
world,
Something secure, around your life to build.

A reflection in a mirror of the way you would like it to be,
Full of dreams and things your eyes cannot yet see.

What's new, things you will see today,
When you are sweeping through your favorite way.

The way you have always gone and are going,
That's Gods way ever flowing.

Like a river moving swiftly, gentle enough to refresh and powerful enough to lift you, Gods generosity, so intense it cannot be described,
Put into words or prescribed.

Pure love, that's what he is,
Judging by righteousness in that heart of his.

God's Child

In winter it usually gets frosty and cold, Today like you it is
strong and bold.

God has blessed it with sunshine and a shower,
Your birthday is a holy hour.

The sun has broken through the norm,
Like you it is loving and warm.

The clouds look like bits of cotton wool as God whispers his
wish from above,
Kindness, goodness and love.

My wish for you is that all day it stays calm and mild, You
deserve it, Gods child.

Brotherly Love

From your mother to your father to your long lost son, Yes it is true, I love the bigger picture of everyone.

For a reason we were put on this earth,
I do not think any less it is worth.

It says in the bible to love your neighbor as yourself,
In marriage, sickness and in health.

If you do this the world will be a better place,
Love will take over in the human race.

What a happy, at ease with each other place it would be, You have heard the saying love makes the world go around and it's true you see.

Billy

When I see couples at Christmas buying presents and going
around the shops,
Pretty little jumpers, vests and tops.

Things for adults and children alike,
Colourful clothes and a BMX bike.

It reminds me of you, how I long for your love and tender
care,
The lasting knowledge that you will always be there.

All this I miss,
I cannot wait for your tender kiss.

Even if the queen stood there, there would be no grater
surprise,
Than to sit and stare into Billy's lovely blue eyes.

Today

Today is the day when your college and university life start,
Today is the day when you are intelligent, positive and smart.

Today is the day when you have just left school and started work,
Today is the day when you have got a new boyfriend and give yourself a perk.

Today is the day when your new baby son has been born,
Today there is a brand new leaf on this new morn.

Today is the day when you listened to Christmas songs like savior's day and mistletoe and wine,
Today is the day where you are on the road to everywhere, another cake on the line.

Today is the day when you make the most of your time on earth,
Today is the day when you celebrate new birth.

Happiness

Happiness is like a pastel pink heart of love, with sugar, cakes and sweets,
Happiness is like the care bears with a different picture that makes them complete.

Happiness is like the boys in college laughing and finding everything that will amuse,
Happiness is like a piece of coconut cake and good news.

Happiness is like a bunch of balloons that you can let off into the sky
Happiness is like when you can have a rest and make cheeses and potato pie.

Happiness is like when you have the freedom to be a nice person and to shine as a woman,
Happiness is like when you have had one Rio drink and want another can.

Happiness is like when you have got rosy cheeks, red lips and cannot stop smiling and having fun,
Happiness is like using stuff from the body shop and us all being the champion of the world like the sun.

Friends

Friends to talk about scented shampoos with, conditioners and shower gel,
Friends to talk about bubble bath who are looking well.

Friends to go out shopping with, trying things on, tops, trousers and white shoes,
Getting some boys after them, having long hair and some good news.

Friends to listen to music with like life is a flower and it's a beautiful life,
Friends to walk down the street with and one day become someone's wife.

Friends to talk about having babies with and enjoying each other's company, sharing experiences and looking forward,
To when the baby is born, all the stuff for it, a pram, a grant and yes I can afford.

Friends in everything, all around, when you are young and flourishing,
Friends that are tops, fashionable and always nourishing.

Jesus Birthday

Jesus birthday is like away in a manger covered in straw and hay,
Jesus birthday with the cattle lowing is a really good day.

All the sheep and other animals keeping Jesus warm,
His mother Mary with her positive heart like most women norm.

The man at the inn, his wife and the Sheppard's coming to see the baby,
Yes this is more than a special child maybe.

With gifts of incense and more, gold frankincense and myrrh,
this was the most blessed baby of all time,
Something that made the chapel bells chime.

With such a gentle face, cute, loving and can make you smile,
The winter sun shining all around him that can last for longer than a little while.

Growing Up

Sometimes when I think of Mrs Jones and how she used to tell us that growing up was an exciting time,
It makes me want to write poems about it that rhyme.

About growing my hair long and having all the boys pay me complements, just starting to get ready for those days,
Still in primary school and getting ready for when I put on some sweet scents and body sprays.

I remember the teacher asking the children where they would see themselves in ten years time, how they would picture themselves,
What sort of work they can imagine themselves doing and where they would place their aspects, what sort of shelves.

I could imagine myself walking down the street, maybe doing office work or having a job as a reporter,
An important role for everybody's daughter.

An important role for everybody and for everybody it will be something different, something that spells success,
Work that helps them to act grown up, develop their adult personality and will impress.

The World

The world is made up of different types of people, different races,
All different shapes and sizes with many faces.

The world is made up of different job industries, differing college courses,
Some English literature, some chemistry, others working with horses.

The world is made up of different animals, some cats, others rabbits, others sheep,
You can dream of all the pampering stuff as you go to sleep.

The world is made up of different cakes, coconut cake, angel cake, lemon drizzle and madeira cake,
They all make you feel brilliant and are there to be admired to make.

The world is made up of different sorts of clothes,
Cardigans, jumpers, hats and scarfs,
Gloves with matching pairs and halves.

Medicine

Sometimes when I go to the chemist where I live or boots in Newport or Cardiff,
I think about different sorts and types of medicines and how they can help, you can have a whiff

Tablets, liquids and injections, medicines you can buy over the counter, on the shelves and by prescription,
Something to thank the NHS for, giving them the right inscription.

Something to be thankful for in general, that you can go and get the medication for whatever condition you might have,
Proper gratitude, being grateful for whatever medicines in this country and abroad that save.

Lifesaving treatments that really do seek a cure for all the ills of the world,
Networks of hospitals and pharmacies that all work together and build.

Establishments, authorities and commitments that will go on for years,
People working together and when successful with unity purrs.

Growing Up Two

Sometimes when I see young girls with long blonde hair or
Barbie girl comes on,
It reminds me of something new getting started, another sweet
song.

Of daisy chains being made and sitting in the sun with your
friends,
Passing the time away till every second ends.

Putting on your favorite tops which let in the sunshine of the
summer,
Of being a woman, delicate, innocent and a newcomer.

The essence of being a woman with string vests, sandals and
putting flowers in your hair,
White blossoms and buttercups with cream being the one your
boyfriend likes.

Months of The Year

January is lonely after Christmas is gone, There will be other things coming up before long.

February's snow lands on the floor,
People are clearing there path outside their door.

March is the time for sowing seeds,
Pretty flowers, no weeds.

It's April, easter is here,
I will be asking my mum for clothes this year.

By May it should be pretty warm,
I will be able to go out in the sun a lot, it is norm.

June is the time for going on holiday,
Somewhere nice wouldn't you say.

July It's time for fun,
There's plenty of things to do in the sun
.

By August the summer is almost over, With leaves burning in the colours of dover.

September concerns fall to the ground,
Some small, some big, all round.

In October I go penny for the guying,
I have to stay out a while and keep on trying.

It's November, bonfire night is soon,
Some of the fireworks seem to go higher than the moon.

The thing about this month December,
Is Christmas that everyone will remember.

Love and Happiness

Love and happiness is every young girls dream,
Love and happiness can make the whole world beam.

Love and happiness can make the whole world smile and
laugh,
Love and happiness can come to animals too like a giraffe.

Love and happiness can mend a family and is for success
stories too,
Love and happiness can make something out of me and you.

Love and happiness can keep you in a job that is steady and
secure,
Love and happiness can hold a family together when it is pure.

Love and happiness comes from seeing people with naturally
sparkly eyes,
Love and happiness cares about what is in the heart that
matters and is wise.

Writing Poetry

Writing poetry like a you girl with long blonde hair, sipping strawberry milkshakes,
With all the new life that it awakes.

Reebok tops and writing poetry up with a positive imagination,
With worlds of rainbow colours and illustration.

Spending money on pastel coloured books,
With plenty of money and new similar looks.

Money to spend on the children in Africa with food and clothes laid out,
White, pastel, rainbow and silver And gold, what it's all about.

More interest coming in to spend on charity all over the world,
More foundations in this place to build.

The song Kiss Me under the milky twilight and riding our bikes,

Riding our bikes in the daylight and staying out all day,
Re-living our youth in the most blissful, calming way.

Mothers and Fathers

Mothers and fathers are really cool,
They buy me sweets and toys and things to go to school.

They give me hugs, kisses and a reason to smile,
Loving arms that stretch out longer than a mile.

Someone who is always there for you, no matter what,
Will care for you and love you a lot.

You will never get another,
Like your father and mother.

They are your best friend,
Always ready to sort out and mend.

God Is

God is like the sun shining through the trees when I look up
at the sky,
God is like the beauty of nature, rice and rye.

God is like the spring, out of every comer in spring life will
sprout,
God is the everlasting life, something we cannot do without.

He starts off as a seed and then grows in our heart,
He bonds us to him till it is impossible to part.

To feed on God, sing his praises and prayer,
Are all important for us to share.

That our soul may rejoice in the gospel for ever more,
Pointing up to the sky without one flaw.

Everlasting Love

Sometimes when I daydream and see the doves on high, I think about God as I look up to the sky.

I think about him wanting us after all we have done, Love us enough to give his son.

We can understand it because we are also forgiving, God's love proves that he is living.

His alive in charity work that people do,
The happy nature of me and you.

He is the splendor of the sky as I see the clouds
floating through the air,
The everlasting wonder that will always be there.

He makes it easy for us to understand,
He will always be there to give us a helping hand.

He is the one who gave us life and loved us first, Overflowing with love and ready to burst.

He is the one who is worthy of and deserves our praise, He is the one who understands us all and will amaze.

The Beauty of Nature

Sometimes as I am walking home from school or going to a country place,
I see the world as it should be, full of grace.

I see young boys and girls going after each other and sharing romance,
Horses in the fields that seem to dance.

Things that I see around me every day,
It is only when you look that beautiful things come to bay.

Like the sun shining through an oak tree or on a young girls hair,
Something that will always be there.

It is the mystery of the countryside and natural food that grows,
Pretty flowers all in rows.

Fields that seem to stretch for miles, Beauty that brings wonder into smiles.

The old telling stories to the young,
Children playing hide and seek through the gooseberry bushes and having fun.

A proper family with a mum, dad, sister and brother, Man and nature living in harmony with each other'

Things that make you want to praise God more and more,

Curiosity that opens up a new door.

A Mothers Love

A mothers love is special like nothing you have ever experienced before,
The bond between mother and child grows more and more.

Because you are a part of them and they are a part of you,
It's like taking something old and making it new.

A mothers love is warm and tender,
When you could do with feeling well, it puts you on a mender.

When you are not confident and have nowhere else to run,
A mothers love stretches out her arms and says come here Hun.

A mothers love is like the darling buds of May, you have only got one mother,
Who you should never turn away from or want to swop for another.

Young Girl

Sometimes when I see a young girl going into a clothes shop or buying shampoo,
It reminds me of when I was that age and had nothing else to do.

When I could walk through the country with the sun still shining through my long hair,
Enjoying the beauty of nature without a care.

Going along to brownies and then up to girl guides,
On a horse of purity and innocence she rides.

In her room is the fragrant sent of flowers,
Adventures and stories that last for hours.

Young girl who's youth never fades away, her beauty always flourishing like an ever flowing stream,
So fresh, every boys dream.

Life

Life can be good if it is mapped out from the beginning,
When you are a teenager you keep on winning.

When you are in the flower of your youth and have long hair
down your back,
Planned out in front of your face onto the best rack.

Then there is what you want your children to be like and how
well you want them to do,
Get a good job, maybe their own business too.

When they are all grown up and have children of their own,
Your pastimes and their interests which are all in tone.

Your family making a success story of their lives all the way,
To have a brighter, better day.

Freedom

We all have the right to our freedom, to go out and have lots
of boyfriends, to have children, to get engaged or married,
To spread our eggs out in as many baskets as possible and
have them carried.

To maybe have a nanny who can help you to look after your
children till they are old enough to get a good job,
Set up their own business, do a bit of cooking and put on the
hob.

Freedom to get your poems published, set up your own white
Persian cat business and white rabbit business,
Freedom to breed them all over the world and say yes.

Freedom to marry a billionaire and to save billions of people
in Africa and all over,
Freedom to make needy places like the fields of dover.

Listening

Sometimes when I am in school and there is a song, listen with
your eyes and sing everything you see,
It reminds me of an innocent child's rainbow and the children
can sing along with me.

There is something about listening that makes me think,
Seeing the five year old's have a Ribena drink.

Seeing them listen twice as much as they talk,
The teachers telling them to eat with a knife and folk.

The teachers looking out for them and looking after them and
making sure they listen,
The orange squash they are drinking starting to glisten.

The food they are eating doing them good and making them
big and strong,
The way they are listening to have a job, one day it will not
be long.

Colours

Colours are brilliant, colours are the best,
They are full of wonder and summer zest.

They are full of love and happiness and reflect different types
of emotion,
You can make different types of innocent drinks out of them,
body butters and lotion.

You can get children's clothes in all the colours of the
rainbow,
They are all beautiful and some of them flow.

They all can bring out the fruits of the Holy Spirit in all of us,
with many different shades and tones,
Sweets, lolly pops and ice cream cones.

Milk shakes and cakes of different colours and flavors,
The new bright vitality of teenage ravers.

CPSIA information can be obtained
at www.ICGtesting.com
Printed in the USA
BVHW062014210622
640289BV00015B/1597

9 781398 433274